A Love Story

Poems of God's Eternal Love

by

Regina Marie Blaylock

DORRANCE PUBLISHING CO
EST. 1920
PITTSBURGH, PENNSYLVANIA 15238

The contents of this work, including, but not limited to, the accuracy of events, people, and places depicted; opinions expressed; permission to use previously published materials included; and any advice given or actions advocated are solely the responsibility of the author, who assumes all liability for said work and indemnifies the publisher against any claims stemming from publication of the work.

All Rights Reserved
Copyright © 2018 by Regina Marie Blaylock

No part of this book may be reproduced or transmitted, downloaded, distributed, reverse engineered, or stored in or introduced into any information storage and retrieval system, in any form or by any means, including photocopying and recording, whether electronic or mechanical, now known or hereinafter invented without permission in writing from the publisher.

Dorrance Publishing Co
585 Alpha Drive
Suite 103
Pittsburgh, PA 15238
Visit our website at www.dorrancebookstore.com

ISBN: 978-1-4809-4554-8
eISBN: 978-1-4809-4577-7

Dedication

My Jesus

Thy hands

Thy feet

Thy heart

Five roses for thee!

(This poem was written to go with a cross my aunt painted. On the cross are five roses to represent the wounds of our Lord.)

This book is dedicated to my children. I pray that they continue to walk close to God the rest of their lives. I hope they dream big dreams and learn the love of God is like no other.

Introduction

This collection of poems has been written over nine years. They are about walking closer with God and learning about love from him. If we dream big dreams and walk close to him through his love, we will be calmer and balanced. God's amazing love is all around us, especially during difficult times.

This book is divided into the different ways God showed his love to me. In my journey of the loss of my home and the separation of my family, I realized without the love of one another we are nothing. The things we love to do have no meaning. Our desire to do good for others and to show love to others is our existence.

To know the deepest love of God happens when he picks us up from our falls. To walk with him helps us see life more compassionately. To let go and trust in the Lord is true faith. Then you will know God's eternal love. From this you will know love like you have never known it before.

Revelation is the realization that God is alive, walking amongst us through Jesus. We find him in the deepest part of our hearts. We are the people of God, and we should walk upright in the strength of God through faith. This is the deeper walk with God I share with others through this collection of poems—"A Love Story" of God's neverending love for us.

Contents

Chapter 1:   My Life 1

Chapter 2:   God's Love 25

Chapter 3:   Compassion 47

Chapter 4:   Rescue Me 59

Chapter 5:   How Does God Knock on Your Door? 77

Chapter 6:   God Nurtures and Guides 97

Chapter 7:   Only You, My King 113

Chapter 8:   Sing to Me, You Angels 127

Chapter 9:   To My Love 137

Chapter 10: Symbols of God's Love 159

Chapter 11: Family 173

Chapter 12: Revelations 189

Chapter 1
My Life

The poems in this chapter are about my journey with God through very heart-wrenching times. I've lived through a divorce, helping my children through the death of their father, losing our home, being separated from my children, and being reunited with my children. The poem "They See Money" is about how people judged me after the death and funeral of my children's father.

The poem "Without Love" is about the darkness, loneliness, and numbness I felt when I lost my home and my children and I were apart. "A Letter to My Adversaries" is a poem God helped me to write to stand up strong to others who have wrongly judged me.

"Shine" is about how God made me see I was beautiful and loved eternally. He helped me stand up again.

> Psalms 45:1-2: "Beautiful words fill my mind as I compose this song for the king. Like the pen of a good writer my tongue is ready with a poem. You are the most handsome of men, you are an eloquent speaker. God has always blessed you."

God has blessed me forever.

My Life

My life is filled with
Quiet moments
Peace & Love
No great big house
No fancy car
Just my daughter and I
With our loving Daisy
My life is filled with
A quiet contentment
Knowing God's here
Leading the way
Giving me beautiful poems
About life & love
Teaching me many lessons
Of family and friends
My life…right now
Is quiet
But many rainbows and
Promises are unfolding
In this quiet place
I believe…
He has touched me
My life is…
Just beginning
In this quiet place

Without Love…

If not Love
I have nothing
My heart beats
I look around &
See God's work
Everywhere
But without His Love
I am nothing
For it is God
Who picked me up
And dried off my tears
Not man
He held me tight
Both day & night
He was there
When they shunned &
Chastised me
He held me close &
Shielded me from
The bruises of the stones
He coveted me
Surrounding me with Angels
Guiding me through a
Fierce, Fiery Furnace
When I was blinded &
Could not see
He showed me the way
He directed me around
The snares of the enemy
Jesus walked beside me

He held my hand
He showed me how
To stand up strong to those
Who persecuted me
He taught me…
Triumphant Faith…
He walks with me
He shows me the way
To live a life of
Faith, not Fear
I am becoming
Stronger and wiser
He gives me many lessons
Some very difficult to learn
But He is patient
He walks in a Steady Stride
He picks me up when I fall
He dries off my tears
He teaches me and guides me
On the path He has chosen
His will…will be done
No man can thwart the
Plans of Jesus
He shields me from others
Who do not understand
He shelters my children
And brings us to a new land
For He has chosen me
For an extraordinary Life
He wants all of it to
Bring my life
Deeper meaning and

To bless others
Through His work in me
My stride is becoming
Steadier
My fears have become less
My heart is becoming
Full of gratitude and joy
He wants me to be
Happy
He promises great joy
He sits beside me
In His Eternal Garden
And teaches me tiny lessons
And reveals many truths
But He loves me so…
And this I know
For He is patient and kind
And loving beyond compare
He will always be with me
For all is not as we see
He tenderly guides me
Along a vast sea
To my home in the
Heavens
Where He will be
Waiting for me!

They See Money

They see money…
They don't see me
I bought a home
For my family to
Grow up and be safe
And warm
God helped me right a
Terrible wrong that was
Done to us
But they didn't see our pain
Or our hurting
They saw a big house
A new car
They saw money
They didn't see us
Trying to follow God
And heal
Joy and peace surrounded us
From God above
We were happy together
Serving God
But they didn't see us
They saw a nice bike
A basketball hoop
A nice doll
They didn't see the
Prayers in the middle of
The night
For God to protect us
From the threats

They didn't see the confusion
They didn't hear the music
For God to help us
Journey on
They saw the flowers
They saw the vacations
They saw the dancer
They saw the soccer player
They didn't see us
And when greater loss
Struck us
They didn't see the pain
They didn't see the confusion
They didn't catch the tears
Raining down in the night
They saw the people with money
Who tried to soften the blows
They saw a rich church
They saw money
They didn't see us
They didn't see the pain
In my son's eyes as
They handed him
The memorial flag
They saw wealth
And when we brought home
The material things
A lost soul left behind
They saw a large television
They saw big speakers
They saw cool guitars
But they didn't hear

The cries in the night
They didn't find out
About the lies
That were stabbing us
They didn't see the
Embarrassment
To find all the women
Involved
To find out
We were a joke
They saw new coats from
A ski store that
Righted a wrong
They saw a trip taken
To ease the pain and to
Prepare us for another
Agonizing event full of pain
All of this occurring over our
Birthdays
They saw things
They saw money
When we turned to family
To surround us during healing
They saw trips
They saw money
When the children
Had great successes
After so much pain
We were met with
Jealousy and revenge
We were met with denial
Of family members

We were met with fear
That we might want
Money
When we were separated
We tried to keep
Some form of family
We were hurting
We were in great pain
Tears rained from
Our faces
Numbness…
As time went by
And people were worried
We might want…
Money
They expressed how much
Of a burden we were
On them
They saw…money
They saw vindication
They were…
Satisfied
With their revenge
Although we helped
So many throughout
Our many heartbreaks
We were met with
Chastisement,
Satisfaction…
That we lost our home
No one saw a family
No one saw the pain

No one saw the rain
Pouring down on us
No one saw…us
They just…
Saw…
 Money!

A Letter to My Adversaries

Today I saw
God's hand at work
A beautiful blessing
Saved a family's home
And secured their future
Today I received
Two hugs
One from a heart untrue
Pretending
But not sincere
Today I received a hug
From a true heart
Who sensed my pain
But God has silenced me
I cannot say anything
A hug needed…
Tears rained down my face
As I drove homeward
For God said,
"Ask for help!"
But help was not granted
To me due to mistrust
In their hearts
Because of gossip
They believe to be true
I pray for my day of
Justice
But that is in
God's hands

The feelings are real
The numbness and disappointment
I felt in those that I helped
Only chastised me
If I could say something
To my adversaries
All I would say is:
I am here
I am not stupid
I am not crazy
I am loving and kind
But no one noticed
I love my children
I stood up against
My persecutor
And saved our lives
That I stood strong
All the while
Helping others
Serving God as a family
Surrounding them with
The love of my
Extended family
But no one saw us
As a Family
No one believed our story
No one saw
When we were hurting
They didn't live it….
We did
But we are strong
Through Christ

We are still standing
Compassionate and Loving
Wiser
We are a Family
God loves and protects us
He will never fail us
We are here,
We are a family
We have feelings
We are not
Nothing
So when you see us
Walking together
Hold your tongue
Keep your gossip
To yourself
For we have walked
Through a mighty storm
We have felt the
Pain
It was real and
The tears came down
Like rain
We have suffered
Much loss
But we are here
We are a family
We still give to others,
Love one another,
And believe in God.

Balanced

Today I feel secure
At peace and loved
For God has settled
My fears and anxiety
He holds me tight
All through the night
When I toss and turn
Because I feel
Something is not right
Today I am calm
For all is quiet now
My heart is not
In turmoil
I know the promises
He has revealed
Are more than I
Could have ever dreamed
Today I am balanced
I am deeply loved
By my Savior
Jesus Christ
Today I am not sad
Or in despair
I know He holds
The key
For healthier and happier
Tomorrows
Today I am balanced
Alone and not afraid
Today my Savior

Sits quietly, holding my hand
And Bluebirds and Rainbows are
About the land
Today I am balanced
I do not grieve for
Lost loved ones
For He has shown me
There is eternal life
And I will be with
Them again
Today I am balanced
I do not have to
Hide in shame
For my Savior
He loves me
I know I am not
To blame
Evil men have hurt me
And destroyed my reputation
But God has stepped in
Not a word has
He spoken
He is cleaning up
The messes
He has chastised
The wrong
He has vindicated
My honor
Cast out the evildoers
My God will not
Forsake me
He has taught me

Wise lessons
So today,
I am happy
For He loves me
So dearly…
Today I am balanced

Shine
(a song)

Shine for others to see
How much you mean
To me
Shine bright
Follow your inner light
Shine, Shine,
Shine on
For all is going to
Be beautiful
Don't hide your light
It is too bright
Don't hang your head
Don't think & dread
Of bad things
Believe
The world is beautiful
Shine, Shine
Shine on
For you have
What it takes
To bring happiness
To others
Let your heart glow
Walk close to me
So others will see
How I have shaped thee
Shine, Shine,
Shine on
Beauty is from within

The past is over
The best is yet
To come
So begin to
Shine, Shine
Shine on
For you are beautiful
You are full of love
Be kind
Walk in peace
Show the world
That strife will cease
When you walk
With me
Shine, My beautiful Daughter
Shine,
Shine,
Shine on.

Chapter 2
God's Love

These poems are about God's eternal love. He is so patient and kind. Even when God is quieting our hearts and caressing our souls, He is teaching us to be wiser and more compassionate. When we have trying times, He reminds us He loves and cares about us. He settles our hearts and heals our souls. "In My Father's Arms" and "Shower Me" are about this.

Love is a gift from God. "Zaviear" is about a child who barely began life when he was stricken with a virus that changed him from a normal baby into a severely disabled baby. Yet he gave so much love and happiness to others.

> Psalms 98:1-3: "O sing unto the Lord a new song; for he hath done marvelous things: His right hand, and his holy arm, hath gotten him the victory. The Lord hath made known his salvation: his righteousness hath he openly shewed in the sight of the heathen. He hath remembered his mercy and his tructh towards the house of Israel: all the ends of the earth have seen the salvation of God."

God's greatest gift is love.

Jesus Reminds Me

Love is Patient
Love is Kind
Love is not Boastful
Love is not Envious
Love endures all things
Love is the essence
Of Mankind
A true heart
Loves without
Judgment
Be kind
Love others as
I have loved you
Your cup will
Runneth over

Believe in the Father

Believe in
The angels
They protect and help
Guide you
Believe in the
Holy Spirit
It wraps a cloth
Of protection and faithfulness
Around you
Believe in
Your guardian angel
She is steadfast and true
Believe in
The miracles
For amongst them is
You
Believe in
The strength
Of my love and
Tender care
For it protects you
From all evil and
Steers you away from
The snares
Believe in
The Gospel
And the Father Most High
For He is your Savior
That brought you
Out of despair

Believe in
The riches of a
Faithful and loving heart
Believe in
The Gold
That a family imparts
There are no riches
Of earth that compare
To the love of
The Father
For a heart in despair
So rise up and smile,
Be kind and take heart
For today you are saved
And from your Father
You will never part

God Loves Me
(song)

He touches my
Heart every day
From out of the blue
A smile and a hug
The sound of laughter
The voice of a tiny tot
Welcoming me
Yes, God loves me
He caresses my soul
He soothes my fears
Every day a new blessing
Is revealed
And my perceptions are
Shown to be false
Oh, my God
How He loves me!
With a grateful heart
I thank him
For each and every day
I can breathe out
And breathe in
And when that
Enormous Mountain appears
Right before my eyes
He walks me through it
And as I turn to say goodbye
He gives me His love

And strength
To see the hopes and beauty
Of tomorrow
Yes, how my God
He loves me!

Contentment

Be quiet
Lean into me
Breathe in…
Breathe out…
Let go!
Trust
I will bring
Everything you need
You will have
Balance again
In your life
Peace, love, and joy
Are on the horizon
Be content
I will bring
Blessings each
New day
Stop rushing about
For you are missing
Many blessings
Walk peacefully
With a loving heart
Lay all your burdens
At my feet
Breathe in…
Breathe out…
Let go!
A spark will ignite and
Glorious blessings
And many miracles

Will abound
Now, settle down
My child
Release the grudges and
Injustices
Sit a while in
The garden of my
Kingdom with me
No rushing here
Just life
It goes on without
The hustle and bustle
Of to-do lists
My child, rest a while
And smile
Let your heart be light
Be content
I will do the rest!

Love

Love is kind
Love is Beautiful
Love is untouched
Love sparkles and shines
For all to see
Love is not haughty
Or showy
Love is humble
Love never hurts those
Who show their heart
Love is of God
Love is angelic
It is pure and
White as snow
Love knows no bounds
Love abounds
From person to person
Love shows how
Precious life is
Love is a beauty
All its own
It is deep in fragrance
And color like a beautiful
Red rose
Love is crimson red
Like the blood spilled
To protect another's life
Love caresses and heals
The wounds of the heart
Love is life

A smile or a hug is a remedy
That shows hope and
Dissolves despair
Love is not glorious
And powerful like
The wealthiest
Royalty of the world
Love is the
Sparkling eyes of a
Newborn baby
Love is the
Peace and tranquility
Of a setting sun
Love is the shimmers
And shining of stars
Speckled across a
Clear night sky
Love is the
Promise of each new day
As the birds
Begin to chirp
As the sun rises on
The horizon of each
New day
Love is the cleansing
Of a fresh spring rain
Where life pops up
From the fertile soil
Love is the colorful display
Of a double rainbow
After a thunderstorm
Love promises

Never to forsake us
Love is hope, kindness,
And the promise
Of timelessness
And unending cycles of life
Love nurtures and guides
Love is the promise
That there is
Eternal life
And death
Is just a myth
Love
The greatest gift
Bestowed upon us
By one who walked
This land
To give us
Eternal life

He Came...

He came as a
Meager poor man
Earning a living
With His hands
And with strife
As he grew in
The nurturing light
Of His Father
He showed others
A steadfast
Faith of
Following the Father
He was tortured
And mocked
And died a gruesome
Death
But His heart
Was with His
Father and
The will His Father
Gave Him to fulfill
Today we walk
With true hearts
That show the
Glory of God
When they are
Open and walking
With the Father
A gift of freedom
Given at great

Sacrifice
From one whose love
Is the True Love
Of the world
Blessed be His name!

Shower Me

Shower me with love
From above
Shine your light
Through my heart
For others to see
Shower down the
Water I thirst for
Let me catch it
On my face
Shower kisses and hugs
Tug on my heart
With them
Shine your spiritual
Light
Upon me in the night
Shower grace, mercy,
And peace
To guide me in
My darkest hour
Shower me from above
All of your
Love
So I can share your heart
With those searching
To start
Walking with thee
Shower me
Oh, Lord,
With your Love
From above.

In My Father's Arms

I am calm
Warm and loved
Here in my Father's arms
No worries
No weight
He holds me
Close to His heart
I am comfortable
No wants
No needs
Here in my Father's arms
I feel His
Deep love for me
I have peace
No yearnings
No tears
No pain
Here in my Father's arms
I know everything
Is taken care of
He will provide
He will never leave me
He walks with me
Teaching me of
His wondrous works
Here, in my Father's arms
Everything makes sense
Everything is balanced

He answers my questions
And helps me heal
Content
Here in my Father's arms.

Zaviear

A beautiful gift
Sent to us from God
You taught us compassion
And the true meaning of love
Your precious smile
And your dramatic
Deep brown eyes
Melted our hearts
The warmth of your smile
And the presence of
Your love
Brought all of us
Closer together
Zaviear
You lived a short life
But a powerful life
Showing all of us
The true meaning
Of life and love
Zaviear, an angel
Returning to heaven

Chapter 3
Compassion

When we lost our home, we were evicted. My neighbors and church helped move everything out of my house. My neighbor Missy and her daughter Alex offered to let my daughter stay with them so she could finish out the school year. Many people showed compassion that day. But in the days and months to come, I received much chastisement. But Missy stayed strong and let my daughter stay with her family. I was trying to keep my son in college and let my daughter finish dance so she wouldn't lose many of her friends. We had two cars that needed repairs. People talked to me like I didn't know how to add up the money or budget, but with several pay cuts and the loss of income when my son turned eighteen it put me in jeopardy quickly. I learned once you put your money in a 401k, it is difficult to get it out. I had money in a 401k that I couldn't retrieve. So I sat tight, living with family members off and on until I could find an apartment to reunite us. It was very hard. Every time I went to stand up, something put me back down. I needed money, but no one thought I could handle it. They didn't worry about that when I donated to the church or when I saved a family member's home.

All through this time, I observed Missy and the worry all over her face for my daughter and me. Finally, with God's help, we found a place to live and were reunited. I have not been able to thank Missy for all that she and her family did for us. It is kind of embarrassing. These poems are dedicated to Missy and Alex, who showed deep compassion when others stood by and judged.

Psalms 46: "God is our refuge and strength, a very present help in trouble."

A Letter to Missy

I thank God each day
For your deep, compassionate
Heart
You were there to help me
When I desperately needed help
Your giving heart
Cared for my daughter
At a time of great loss
In times like these
The most important thing
We need is Love
You gave my daughter
The love and compassion
She needed to persevere
Through those difficult times
Thank you for being
A friend
That goes beyond

Hearts of Gold

Hearts of Gold
Pick you up
When you are down
Never waver
When chaos is abounding
Hearts of Gold
Are deep with compassion
They rescue and nurture
Those wounded and alone
In the world
Hearts of Gold
Know how to serve God
They show love
In everything they do
Hearts of Gold
God is watching you!

Kindness Is All Around

Kindness is all around
Look and see
Someone is watching thee
Picking up the broken pieces
Rebuilding after destruction & loss
Kindness is all around
Look and see
Peek around the corner
And you will see
Someone giving hope to others
A watchful eye
Knows when you cry
Kindness is all around
Look and see
A smile and a hug
To let someone know
They are loved
Kindness is all around
Look and see
This I have found
Picking up those who are down
So do not frown
For God is watching over thee
Kindness is all around

Alex
Dedicated to Alexandra Deahl

Caring & Loving
Wisdom beyond your years
Friendly & Kind
You are a true friend
Standing Strong
And never wavering
When someone needs you
Alex
Beautiful inside & out
You know
How to
Walk like…
Jesus

You Were There
Dedicated to Melissa Deahl

I was lost
And all alone
The heavy burden
I could no longer carry
You were there
You did not have to come
You gave me a hug
That gave my heart a tug
You came
You didn't have to
You opened your heart
You offered to help
You saw my worry
You saw my fear
You helped me
You offered a home
To my daughter
You were there
It wasn't easy for you
But you came
You helped
It wasn't easy
I could see
How much you cared
It was written
All over your face
I struggled and wept
In the night
For God to show me

The light
In the darkness
But you helped
You were there
Others just stopped
To stare
Some gossiped and snickered
Some cursed and scorned
But you carried on
You were there
You cared
You showed love
You showed compassion
You shared
Thank you
For persevering and
Praying
For I was lost and
In great pain
And you were there
To help in the storm
You eased the pain
For when everything
Seemed grim
You stepped in
You were there

Chapter 4
Rescue Me

In this chapter and throughout this book, you will read poems that are songs. Many times when we are hurting, we cry out to God to rescue us from the burdens we cannot bear. "Rescue Me" is a song God gave to me when I cried out for him. He gave me many songs to dry off my tears.

> Psalms: 33:1-4: " Rejoice in the Lord, O ye righteous: for praise is comely for the upright. Praise the Lord with harp: sing unto him with the psaltery and an instrument with 10 strings. Sing unto him a new song ; play skillfully with a loud noise."

When God comes, He sends us His love. "I Am Sending Out My Love" is a time when he was reassuring me of his love and that he had not forsaken me. During difficult, hurting times, it is hard to see in the darkness. "Never Believe" is God telling us all is not lost.

Rescue Me
(song)

Every night
On my knees
I pray
God, come rescue me
I hear your name
I call to you
Come rescue me
On my knees
I pray
My heart will say
God, come hear
Me pray
My heart will say
God, come rescue me
From where I have
Gone astray
I need you
Here
God
On my knees
I pray
God, come rescue me
Come hear me pray
I need your love
I need you near
In close to here
On my knees
I pray
God, come rescue me

My heart will say
Come rescue me
I need you near
For I have fear
Upon my knees
I cry out to you
Come hear me
Pray
God, come rescue me
I know that you
Are near
I am right here
On my knees
I pray
Hear my heart
Cry out
In pain
Lord!
Come rescue me!
From heaven above
You have
Rescued
Me!

Untitled

God is good
God is love
He sends down
Blessings from above
He holds me tight
In the night
And wakes me with
The bright morning
Sunlight
All my fears
Have disappeared
Standing strong
No one can see
How long
I have waited
Anticipated
The coming of
My True Love
God is good
God is love
He sends me
Blessings
From above
No longer do
I wake
In fear
And shake
For I know my
God is here
I can no

Longer fear
I look up above
I know that
I am loved
Things from
The past
Will not last
For angels
Sing
To me in the night
God brings me
Joy and laughter
Happily ever after
For I know
The King lives
In my heart
He changes the world
In the silence
I feel His
Presence
As He guides me
Down a road
I bear no load
For my Savior
Lives
He always gives
I am blessed
He cleaned up
A mess
My heart is
Filled with joy
For He lives

In Me
And others will see
As my life unfolds
How close the
Father holds me
In His arms.

I Am Sending Out My Love

I am sending out
My love to you
Beyond the deep blue sea
I am sending out
My love to you
From the mountaintops
I am sending out
My love to you
And it will never stop
My gracious child
Gifts from above
Are abound
For I am sending out
My love for you
My arms will
Wrap around
Joy will come to you
Beyond compare
I am sending out
My love for you
From everywhere

God's Tender Gift

Love is a tender gift
God gives
Each of us
He wants us to know
His immense
Love for us
If we can understand
His love
Then we will not
Be searching
For something
We feel we have lost

When we understand
God's love
And open our hearts
To receive it
Deep within
We have peace
And we are content
God never gives up
On showing us
His Love

Believe

Believe
My child
Believe
I am your Savior
Believe
Good things are
Coming your way
Believe
I am in control
Of all things
Believe
I chose you
To walk this path
Believe
You are worthy of
My eternal love
Believe
You are worthy of
A true love
Steadfast in my light
In my love
Believe
In impossible dreams
Believe
You will do
Great things
Believe
Before the dawn
Of each day
I can hear you pray

Believe
In the night
I am not
Out of sight
Believe
The pitter-patter
Of little feet
You will soon greet
Believe
In happiness and love
Believe
All these things
Come from above
My dearest daughter
Believe
All things will
Come to be
Because you
Believe in me
Believe!

Each Day

Sometimes life can be crazy
Sometimes life can be calm
Each day has its own beginnings
When the light dawns
Each day has its challenges,
Frustrations, and rewards
Each day has its endings
When the sun goes down
Cast all your cares upon me
Collect only sweet memories
For each day has its own
Beginnings and endings
Keep only what reminds you
Of Me!

Never Believe

Never believe
That the world
Is at an end
Never believe
That I will
Not come again
Never believe
That people
Cannot see me
Through you
Never believe
You cannot
Have peace
Never believe
That the world
Has no hope
Never believe
That I have
Forsaken you
For I am here
I have given
My life for you
I will never forsake you
I will always
Be true
Never believe
That I will not come
For all has been
Prophesied
I will come again
In the Glory
Of the Lord!

Chapter 5
How Does God Knock on Your Door?

"How Does God Knock on Your Door?" This poem was in response to a statement someone in my small group made about God. She was questioning another's belief in God. Yet God has given her many miracles. Sometimes when God is answering our prayers, we fail to see His miracles.

"Can You Pray" is about how we are the hands and feet of Jesus in this world. There is the loving side of Jesus and the needy side of Jesus. We are the ones who are supposed to help Jesus by caring and giving to one another. Jesus' needy side grows heavier as the world grows colder. "Can you pray to the needy side of the Lord?" means "Will you pray for others? Will you be his hands and feet?"

"Listen in the Quiet" is about quieting our busy minds and taking time to be with God, to listen more and talk less. Just to sit and enjoy the love of God. That is when he can guide you.

> Psalms 22:1: "My God, My God, why hast thou forsaken me? Why art thou so far from helping me, and from the words of my roaring?"

How Does God Knock on Your Door?

You say
Where is God in
This weary world?
I tell you
I am here
When your heart is
Hurting and
Something just isn't
Right
It is me…knocking
Will you let me in?
I want to help
Your heart stop
Hurting
But I must take it
On an adventure
Throughout the world
When you wonder why
Something is
Happening
It is me,
Knocking at your door
Will you let me in?
So I can show
You why and lead
You to help in the
Change
When someone is
Devastated

And destruction is
Appalling
And you wonder
Where is God?
I am right here
When you are so
Frustrated and
You throw your arms
Up in the horror
It is me
Knocking at your door
Will you let me in?
So I can show you
How you can do
Great things
In my name
So there will be
No devastation
Where is God,
You say?
I am right here
Knocking at your door
Will you let me in?
There is so much
Work to be done
In this weary world
Will you open your
Heart to me?
So I can take you
On a journey
Of a lifetime
So I can show you

The purpose for your life
So you can do
Great things!
This is God…
Knocking…
Will you let me in?

Can You Pray
(song)

Can you pray to the
Needy side of the Lord
Oh…oh…
Can you pray to the
Needy side of the Lord
Oh…oh…
For the hungry and the poor
Oh…oh…
Can you pray to the
Needy side of the Lord
Oh…oh…
For all who have hungered
And thirst
Cry out to the Lord
Oh…oh…
Can you pray to the
Needy side of the Lord
Can you free
The burdened and troubled
People
Oh…Lord…
For they have been
Scorned and cast aside
Oh…Lord…
Can you pray to the
Needy side of the Lord
To help those
Hurting and abused
Oh…Lord…
Can you pray to the
Needy side of the Lord

Save this world
From forgotten truths
Oh…Lord…oh…Lord…
Can you pray to the
Needy side of the Lord
Give hope to the
Needy side of the world
Oh…Lord…oh…Lord…
Give strength to the
Needy side of the world
Oh…Lord…oh…Lord…
Give love and peace
To the needy side of the world
Oh…Lord…oh…Lord…
Cast your hands to the
Needy side of the world
Oh…Lord…oh…Lord…
For through you all things
Dead become real
Oh…Lord…oh…Lord…
Can you pray to the
Needy side of the Lord
Help someone who has
Fallen into darkness
Oh…Lord…oh…Lord…
Bring those cast out
Into the light
Oh…Lord…oh…Lord…
Can you pray to the
Needy side of the Lord
Oh….oh….

You'll Find Jesus
(song)

You'll find Jesus
You'll find Jesus
You'll find Jesus
Just the way
You thought He would be
You'll find Jesus
You'll find Jesus
You'll find Jesus
Looking down and
Watching over thee
You'll find Jesus
You'll find Jesus
You'll find Jesus
Singing into all of the
Hope and love for thee
You'll find Jesus
You'll find Jesus
You'll find Jesus
Looking for all
Of the possibilities
You'll find Jesus
You'll find Jesus
You'll find Jesus
Standing right in front of thee
You'll find Jesus
You'll find Jesus
You'll find Jesus
Singing lullabies to thee
You'll find Jesus

You'll find Jesus
You'll find Jesus
Walking right beside thee
You'll find Jesus
You'll find Jesus
You'll find Jesus
Coming down to save thee
You'll find Jesus
You'll find Jesus
You'll find Jesus
Bringing many blessings to thee
You'll find Jesus
You'll find Jesus
You'll find Jesus
Carrying out all of His promises to thee
You'll find Jesus
You'll find Jesus
You'll find Jesus
Coming up and loving thee
You'll find Jesus
You'll find Jesus
You'll find Jesus
Open up your heart to thee!

In My Father's Arms #2

In my Father's arms
I lay to rest
He holds me tight
He knows me best
In my Father's arms
Is where I want to be
So I can dream
Impossible dreams
Although it seems
Unreal to thee
I know when He is
Nearest me
In my Father's arms
I lay
Content and quiet
I will stay
Until the dawn
Of His bright sunlight
I am nurtured
And loved
Throughout the night
In my Father's arms
I'll always be
He knows me
He comforts me
In my Father's arms
My heart is closest
To thee
He loves me so
I'll never know

How deep
How strong
His love flows
In my Father's arms
Complete...I am
My beauty
And His gentleness
I am the one
He shapes and molds
To do great things
I am told
In my Father's arms
I will always be
He holds me like
No other can
In my Father's arms
Peace and love
Dreams of hope
And endless love
I wake to the silence
Of the first dawn's light
I have been
Nurtured and loved
All through the night
In my Father's arms
I want to be
But, until eternity
I will walk with thee
In my Father's arms
Nurtured and loved
Complete in His eyes
There will be no surprise

In my Father's arms
Behold I lie
Until the day I die
When He will
Pick me up
And hold me tight
I will rise and live
In His bright sunlight
In my Father's arms
I am blessed
He fills my heart
With His promises
As I journey home
I know I can rest
In my Father's arms
I am truly blessed!

Listen in the Quiet

Listen in the quiet
For I am here
Waiting for you
To talk to me
I have much to
Tell you
I have much
To teach you
Lean on me
Open your heart
And let the spirit
Hear my every word
For I am walking
With you
Every step you take
I am there
Do not rush off
In a hurry
Sit a while…
And listen
There is so much
I want to show you
Listen, my child
Listen in the quiet

God Made You

God made you
In your heart
God made you
It's just the start
God made you
A part of Him
God made you
You're willing
To start anew
That's why God made you
God made you
Within your heart
You are a part of Him
Willing to start anew
Believe in all
He can do
Because you brought
Your heart to Him
God made you
Believe in all
He can do
You're willing to start anew
For all He has
Is yours
Begin to embrace
The new life
He has created for you
Before you had
Gone astray
But now you

Live and believe
In all He has to say
Walking with Him
You are beginning to
Live the life
He created you to live
That's why
God created you anew
Believe in all
He can do
Because all that see you
Walk through the
Heavenly Gates so blue
God made you
To start anew
Believe in all
He can do
He recreated you
To start becoming
A true believer
Of all He can do
All will be anew
God created you
To bring a special gift
He brought you
Walking hand and hand
He believes you
Can do all things
He created you to do
Do not become
Soooo…blue
He created you

In His image
To do great things
So…
God created you
So new
To carry out
A special purpose
Only He believes
You can do
So God made you!

Chapter 6
God Nurtures and Guides

The poem "Beautiful Dreamer" is about how God plants seeds in our hearts that we feel we must follow. Sometimes we don't know why. God wants us to realize the dreams he has for our lives. But these dreams aren't little dreams. They are Big Dreams! He opens the door of our dreams when we persevere.

"A Flower in the Sunshine" is about how God loves us. How when others have unflattering comments or opinions about how they think we should look or act. God wants us to know he knows perfect because he created all of us perfectly.

"Adversity" is about just that. Following your heart and not listening to others' negative comments but persevering to reach that dream for your life that God put in your heart.

"Something in Your Heart" is about the seed in your heart that yearns to be with our creator.

> Psalms: 33:20-22: "Our soul waiteth for the lord: he is our help and our shield. For our heart shall rejoice in him, because we have trusted in his holy name. Let thy mercy, Oh Lord, be upon us, according as we hope in thee."

Beautiful Dreamer

Beautiful dreamer
Dream for me
All the wonderful
Things to be
I will grant
Them one by one
As you walk
Under the sun
In my light
And in my love
You will always be
Close to me
Beautiful dreamer
Dream for me
All of the creative
Possibilities
I will change
The world you see
Into rainbows
Just for thee
Beautiful dreamer
In your heart
I placed a seed
Water it with
My words and deeds
And it will
Blossom
For the world to see
That when you
Dream impossible

Dreams
All your wishes
Will be
Beautiful dreamer
My heart reaches
Out to yours
All I have
Will open doors
Beautiful dreamer
I picked thee
To dream up all
These impossibilities
To show the world
I am here
Walking in your
Life
Oh, so near
Beautiful dreamer
Dream for me
All of your heart's
Impossibilities

A Flower in the Sunshine

You are a flower
In the sunshine
Of my love
A beauty to behold
Men stop to
Admire you
Jealous ones try
To pick you
But you are a
Strong, beautiful
Flower
Growing in the
Sunshine of
My love
You adorn the
World
You give pleasure
And hope
To those who are
Searching for me
You are my flower
In the
Sunshine of my love.

He Showers Me with His Love

He showers me with
His love
Rose petals
Line my path
Pain and hurt have passed
He showers me with
His love
I surrender all to Him
He paints
Rainbows in the sky
And washes away
The sorrow in the rain
He showers me with
His love
Smiling faces come
My way
Hugs of joy and
Friendship
Line the road
Of my dreams
He showers me with
His love
As He lulls me
Off to sleep….

Adversity

God is taking me on a
Journey
One that began
Long before I ever knew
I am walking a path
He has laid out for me
Something I've always
Felt in my heart
Others may not understand
The journey I am
Following
Many may judge me
But God will
Always protect me
And guide me
For what is…
Is not what has to be
Sometimes He calls us to
Lead on this journey
So that others may
Learn from our example
It isn't an easy journey
But it is a blessed journey
He teaches those who
Are watching
Along with me
Sometimes I am alone
On this journey
Sometimes He asks me to be
Silent

So His presence
Can be shown
God is taking me on a journey
That will last
'til the end of my days
My story will be told
When my life is
Complete
God has blessed me
And protected me
He is taking me on a
Journey
And I don't want to
Leave His side.

Something in Your Heart

Something in your heart
Cries out to me
Deep within you
There is great joy
Something in your heart
Longs to be with me
To walk with me
To talk with me
Something in your heart
Longs to sit in the silence
And have a conversation
With me
Bring all of your worries
And your questions to me
I am your Father
I will answer them
When you hurt
I will comfort you
When you are confused
I will make things clear
Come to me…
For I am your Father
I have created you
My love for you
Is immense
There is no other
Who knows you
As I do

Live life
Enjoy
Bring everything
To me
I am here!

Something in Your Eyes

Something in your eyes
Twinkles
Something in your eyes
Sparkles and glistens
Something in your eyes
Reveals your heart
Something in your eyes
Reminds me of
Your love
Something in your eyes
Is angelic and pure
Because something in your eyes
Smiles on a stranger
And brings them
Closer to me.

God Leads the Way

God leads the way
So we don't go astray
Get on your knees
And pray
There will be
A new day
When all will see
How to follow me
Through the darkness
Into the light
Follow the path
I have laid out
For thee
For you belong
To me
God leads the way
So we don't
Go astray!

Chapter 7
Only You, My King

Throughout my life, I have had twists and turns on my journey. I was born and raised in the Catholic Church. Then after my divorce, I chose to attend a community church. I wasn't prepared for the adversaries in this church. I was just trying to learn a new way to worship God. He was guiding me. My children and I were healing. We served together in the children's ministry. We also helped and volunteered with other activities. All the while we were being judged. "Critics" is about those opinionated people.

I was unaware that if you were not liked in a community church, they could ask you to leave the church. I was asked to leave four times. Even by people who knew me. One of my favorite childhood movies was *Pollyanna*. In the movie, Pollyanna tells the priest, "Nobody owns a church." I wrote "Nobody Owns a Church" after being asked to leave the church. That is not why God builds a church.

"The Pastor" I wrote about my pastor in the community church I attended because I observed how there were many opinions and directions people wanted to go in the church. He had to discern which ones were important. He had to decide to follow the people or to follow God.

"Only You, My King" is a song I wrote during these times. It is about following God and keeping my eyes on his promises, especially during times of adversity.

Psalms 27:1: "The Lord is my light and my salvation—whom shall I fear? The Lord is the strength of my life—of whom shall I be afraid?"

Only You, My King
(song)

I will worship
Only you, my King
Jesus, you are everything
Tomorrow you will
Sing to me
Everything that's
Heavenly
I bow down here
Upon my knees
Jesus, you are everything
To me
I will worship
Only you, my King
Jesus, you are everything
It's you I only see
Belief and honor
Go to thee
I will worship
Only you, my King
Jesus, you are everything
He is the giver
Of everything
Believe and He will
Always bring hope to those
Who are suffering
Jesus, you are everything
I will worship
Only you, my King
Jesus, you are everything to me

Be strong and try
To carry on
For you only belong
To me
I am your
One and only King
I am all you need
To sing
I will worship
Only you, my King
Jesus, you are everything
To me
I will die and rise
And praise your name
For you are the only one
Who came
To rescue me from
Suffering
Jesus, you are everything
To me
All of my heart and soul
Are now replaced
I've journeyed far
And found your grace
Upon you now
I finally see
Jesus, you are everything
To me
I will worship
Only you, my King
Jesus, you are everything
To me

Serving God

Humbly giving
Of ourselves to others
No repayment
Do we expect
No debt do we repay
Serving God
With an open heart
Unnoticed, quietly
Changing the world
In a quiet moment
When no one is looking
Except
God!

The Pastor

Quiet in nature
A deep love for God
In his heart
He chooses to walk
An extraordinary path
Of faith
Not knowing the future
He steps out to lead
Others who are searching
For a purpose in life
He listens in the quiet
For the guidance
From above
To lead others to
Walk in the
Light and love
For it seems a lonely path
To trust only in God
But it is a rewarding
Life
Raining gifts from above
Touching lives and
Changing the world
On a quiet walk with God.

The Witness

I witnessed the
Power and the glory
Of God's love for me
I have witnessed
A strength
Not seen by any man
I have witnessed
An overwhelming
Kindness and gentle
Caring
My Savior has for me
I have witnessed
His gentle nudges
And sometimes
Strong pushes
In the directions
He has laid out for me
I have witnessed
His reassurance
And shown
His promise
For my life
I have witnessed
God's simple lessons
And how He gently
Teaches and reveals truths
I have witnessed
His gift of life
I have witnessed how
He quietly goes about

Changing wrongs into rights
How He walks into
The darkness and
Picks up the broken
In heart
And walks them into
The light
I have witnessed how
He washes away the sin
Begins a life anew
I stand in awe
For God sees all
I have witnessed
The beauty and love
My Savior has for me
I am His witness.

Critics

Critics pick things apart
They have that
Discerning eye
About them, an air
Of distrust
Resides
Critics steal joy
From the hearts
Of adventurers
They wisp by
And douse
The imaginations
Of dreamers
Critics
Have a difficult life
Their hearts are heavy
Because they
Pass on untruths
And negative opinions
Of others
Critics
Tear down
Instead of
Create.

Nobody Owns a Church

The church is
Not a building
It is the people
Reaching out
Caring and loving
One another
Nobody owns a church
Because…
Nobody owns
God's people
Reach down deep,
Down in your heart
Where God resides
Open up your heart
And God will
Take you on a
Beautiful journey
Bonding with one
Another
As His church
Nobody owns a church!

Chapter 8
Sing to Me, You Angels

There are some people who do not believe in angels, even though angels are written about in the Bible. In the Bible, angels guard and give messages from God. Yet there are still people who do not believe in angels. I believe in angels. The songs and poems in this chapter are from the angels who sang to me in one of my deepest, darkest hours.

> Psalms 15:1-5: "Lord, who shall abide in thy tabernacle? Who shall abide in thy Holy hill? He that walketh uprightly, and worketh righteousness, and speaketh the truth In his heart. He that back biteth not with his tongue, nor doeth evil to his neighbor, nor Taketh up a reproach against his neighbor. In whose eyes a vile person is contemned; But he honoureth them that fear the Lord. He that sweareth to his own hurt, and Changeth not. He that putteth out not his money to usury, nor taketh reward against the Innocent. He that doeth these things shall never be moved."

Sing to Me, You Angels
(song)

Sing to me, you
Angels on high
I love to hear
Your beautiful voices
Sing to me, you
Angels
Watching over me
You comfort me
In my darkest hour
Sing to me, you
Angels
Guarding me through
My trials and tribulations
Sing to me, you
Angels
Giving me hope
Of a new life
Full of peace and prosperity
Sing to me, you
Angels
Let me hear your
Glorious songs
They comfort me
As I dream of
Impossible dreams
Sing to me, you
Angels
Of God's Glory and
Heaven's eternal love

Sing to me, you
Angels
All the rest of
My life
Until I come to
The gates of heaven
To hear your
Ethereal voices and
Join with you in song
Sing…sing…sing…
To me, you
Angels
From Heaven above and
God's eternal love.

I Hear the Angels Sing
(song)

Deep asleep
Snug in my Father's arms
I hear the angels sing
Sweetly they sing
Of beautiful things
Of grace and mercy
And our Eternal King
Serene and blissful
I feel at home and loved
As the angels sing
From up above
I know that here
I do not need to fear
For my Father holds me
Oh, so near
He soothes my soul
And gently caresses my brow
For here there is only
The songs full of love
My heart is peaceful
My soul at rest
For I know I am
Truly blessed
My Father has an
Eternal plan
And He walks with me
In this land
I hear the angels
Surround me in song

As I am lulled to sleep
With such a beautiful melody
I hear the angels sing
Each night
As my Father holds me
Close and tight
For He has created
All that is to be
And He chose me
To follow thee

Sing to the Angels

Sing to the angels
With words of praise
Raise your voice
To the heavens
I am reaching
Out my arms
So that no one
Will come to harm
Spread my love
Throughout the land
Come close to me
And hold my hand
When the world
Seems dark and gray
Do not go astray
Lean into your Father's arms
So I can protect you
From all harm
I am always here
Knock and you will see
The door will open
And your dreams will be
Too many to number
For glorious blue skies
And radiant sunshine
Line a path
To fulfill a purpose
I wrote long ago
On your heart
Your life is important

It is my treasure
Which I cherish
To the ends of the earth
Your purpose for this life
Is written on your heart
It is not about strife
But about love
My love for you and
For everyone your
Life touches
So be kind, be gentle,
Be strong,
Walk in my light and
You will always find
Your way in the night
I am here
Never fear
I am oh, so near
Blessed, Blessed
Be the name of the Lord

Soothing Melodies

Soothing melodies to
Warm your heart
And open it to God
Spiritually guides you
To a higher place
That brings you
Close to me
Settled and peaceful
Your prayer song begins
Glorifying my name
With every thought and prayer
The sounds of songs
Rejoicing my name
Raining down
Blessings from above

Chapter 9
To My Love

During the turmoil of my divorce, I met the love of my life. God brought this person into my life to help show me the lies all around me. He cares for me very much. I first met him at work. I blushed when I was introduced to him. I was quiet and talked very little to him for five years. Then he began asking me about people from my high school he knew. We talked occasionally. After my divorce, he came up to me and told me about his father, who was diagnosed with a terminal illness. He asked me if I knew anything about it. I gave him the information he asked for. Soon we began talking more at work. We saw each other a few times outside of work, but when we became closer something always pushed us apart. I began writing the poetry during this time. I also began being myself. These poems are to my love.

A Love Story

Two hearts locked
Wherever they go
In the world
They yearn for
Each other
Two hearts locked
Unsettled
Unless they are
Together
A love story
Two hearts come
Together
Deny one another
Go searching for
Something
They do not
Understand
A love story
Two hearts lost
Without each other
Searching for a
Meaning in life
Finally find
One another
Two hearts lock
Content
A love story.

Candlelight

The candlelight
Shimmers in the
Darkness
As I wait for you
To come home
Soothing and spiritual
It flickers
When my heart hurts
For the candlelight
In the night
Is shining a
Spiritual light
Asking God to guide
My True Love
To my side
The candlelight
Has romance and
Love at the heart
Of its light
I light the candles
In the darkness
To help my True Love
Find his way to me.

Before the Rising Sun

In the morning
Before the rising of
The sun
I will come
To greet you
In the morning
Before the rising
Of the sun
I will reveal
Myself to you
In the morning
Before
The rising
Of the sun
I will hold you
My beautiful child
And speak to you
There are so many
Plans I have
In store for you
Wait for me
Listen in the
Quiet
I watch over you
In the night
And in the morning
Before the rising
Of the sun
I will talk to you
A beautiful love

Is going to arrive
I will guide both of you
Wait for me
In the morning
Before the rising of the sun.

Send My Love to Another

Send my love
Oh, Lord
To another
This morning
He has journeyed far
Send him my
Warm greetings
And calm his anxieties
Send my love
Oh, Lord
To another
Who has found
His path to you
Help him to be
Strong today
In his convictions
Send my love
Oh, Lord
To another
Who has begun
To walk
With you
Hold his hand today
Help him to smile
And wrap him
In your love
Send my love
Oh, Lord
To another
Your will be done
Oh, Lord

You Make Me Smile

You make me
Smile
I look at you
And I cannot
Frown
For your eyes
Light up
When I enter
The room
Love is written
All over your face
You make me
Smile
When you try
To say something
Witty
When I reply
A deep pink
Blush
Covers your face
And you scratch
Your head
You make me
Smile
When I look at you
And my blue eyes
Make your knees bend
You can't hide
Your love for me
I see every time

You gaze at me
You make my
Heart skip a beat
Nothing needs to
Be said
You look across
The room at me
Your face smiles
Lovingly
I in return
Send a reflection
Of your smile
Back at you
You blush
No fancy dress
No extra makeup
Must I wear
Just my blue eyes
And you smile
You make me
Smile

Kisses

Kisses to say hello
Kisses to say goodbye
Kisses blown across the sky
Kisses of passion
Kisses of tears
Kisses of comfort
Kisses of fear
Kisses to show
What is in your heart
Kisses so long
Never to part
Kisses short and sweet
Kisses that abruptly meet
Kisses of innocence
Kisses of denial
Kisses sooooo soft
And s-l-o-w....
Your face begins
To glow
Kisses

Blue and Brown

You like blue
I like brown
You like the
Deep blue sea
I like the rich
Dark sand
You like a serene
Calm sky
I like the
Moist, dark garden soil
You like the sparkling
Stars in the midnight sky
I like smooth, sweet
Chocolate pudding
You like staring deep
Into my patient blue eyes
I like staring into
Your peaceful, calm brown eyes
I get lost in you….
You get lost in me….
Brown and Blue
Blue and Brown

Almost There

Almost there
We're almost there
Long ago we turned
To the light
That far away
Shined so bright
Now we're almost there
As we toiled and strived
Trying to understand
This life
He took our hands
And walked through
This land
Now we're almost there
He taught us anew
All of the old ways are gone
Memories and songs
Now we're almost there
A bright light
Shines on our faces
And warms our hearts
As we start
All over again
So long it has been
But now we walk
In the light
With He who found us
Lost in the night
And we're almost there
So that we can share

153

Our lives in the sun
We don't have to run
We're almost there
A Promise
A Life
I will become
Your wife
My Love….
We're almost…
There!

My Dearest Love

To my dearest love
Please, I hope
You hear me
For I have much
To say
My heart needs to
Express the Love
I have for you today
I know that you are
Hurting
I know that you
Have great loss
I send my love
So dearly
To comfort you
From this pain
I know that your
Mom was very
Close to you
I know you
Miss her dearly
And wonder what to do
My heart is weeping
Sorrowfully
To know that you
Have such loss
I care for you and
Wish to comfort you
From such pain
I know that she

Inspired you
To walk a stronger walk
She cared for you
And guided you
For many years
'til now
I know the emptiness
You feel
Hurts deeply—none
Compares
I wish I could
Send caring words and
Loving poems to say
She is near you
Every day in such
Beautiful ways
Like when you
Wake to greet the day
She is within the
Silence
As if to say
I love you, son
You're hurting
This pain will go away
For soon you will
Be smiling
And this hurt will fade
Someday
Listen to the Father
Let him guide your
Ways
For soon you will

Find your True Love
And your worries will
Fade away
Happiness and kindness
Will color each new day
Your family will
Be stronger
As He guides you
On your way
A loving wife
Will greet you
All you have to say
I love you!
Please forgive me
For I lost my way
Great Joy and Peace
Await you
But for now I say,
Be at peace, my
Love
Let God guide your way
For I wish to send
My comfort
Through Him
Because only
He knows the way

Chapter 10
Symbols of God's Love

On my first mission trip, I met a young lady who was in the service and engaged to be married. I wrote "The Bride" for her. I wanted to let her know her identity as a person will not fade.

During this time in my life, I was trying to understand what had happened in my life and God revealed many truths. I also learned that with God's help, these are joyous time and they will come again.

"The Rosary" I wrote when God answered my prayer about it I wondered if it was appropriate for me to pray if I was not a practicing Catholic. This poem is the answer to my prayer.

> Psalms 19:1-3: "The heavens declare the Glory of God; and the firmament sheweth his handy work. Day unto day uttereth speech, and; night after night sheweth knowledge. There is no speech or language where their voice is not heard."

The Bride
Dedicated to Jena Camara

Gracious beauty
Pure and delicate in
God's eyes
Your love shines
For all to see
Elegant and charming
Glowing in your
Gown of white
As you walk to meet
Your true love
Rose petals line
Your path
God's love shines on
You today
As you commit your life
To another
Two become one
In His Light
In His Love
Many blessings
Shine on you
From above

The Bouquet

The bouquet is
A symbol of my
Love
For you and how
I pass it on
Through you
Touching many hearts
Reaching out to
Those in need
The bouquet
Is my blessing
For many years
Of happiness
And fruit
I am here
Guiding your love
For one another
Now
And for many years
To come
The bouquet
With its many
Ribbons
Symbolizes my blessings
For your love

Wedding Bells

Wedding bells will ring
For you
My beloved
Your heart yearns
For another
He will be here
At the altar
Of my covenant
Wedding bells will ring
Cross the land
When you and your
True Love joins hands
For when you walk
Down the aisle of
Love
I will be waiting
To bless you
Both
And when that
First kiss
Is upon your lips
Wedding bells will ring
Throughout the heavens
For two have become
One
In the sunlight
Of my love
Wedding bells will chime
And hope will shine
Through your hearts

The Rings

Bound together in
Matrimony
These rings represent
Unending love
You have for
One another
No matter how far
Away you may
Be from
One another
These bands
Tie your hearts
Together in
Love
For when God
Joins two hearts
No man shall
Part them
These rings
Have an endless
Love
For the two of you
That God put
In your hearts
Before you were
Born
Your hearts
Pure and
Untouched were
Destined to be together

From the beginning
As part of
God's plan
These bands
Bind your hearts
No matter where
You are in
This world
Cherish this gift
From above.

The Rosary

Beads strung together
Hope for those who lament
Prayers to God Almighty
Through His pure and holy
Mother
Beads of prayer
Strung in a pattern
Unceasing prayers
The rosary
Each bead represents
The Holy Trinity
Prayers for those
Seeking to find Jesus
Prayers to His Mother
And God on high
Unceasing prayers of lament
Loving hearts
Chant
"Hail Mary,
Full of Grace
The Lord is with thee."
Do not be ashamed
To pray these words
Because with them
I am well pleased
Some say you Idolize
My Mother
But no this is not so
You adore her and respect her
For she is the Mother

Of all Mothers
An example of
God's unending love
Mothers and Women
Throughout the world
The Virgin Mother
Pure as gold
Is here to remind you
How to walk close to me
She is the holiest
Of Holy Mothers
For you to seek to
Pray through her
Pleases the Father
Women of the world
God has not forgotten you
Pray to the Father
Through his Mother
The Virgin Mary
For you carry
The burdens of the
Future of the world
As you pray,
"Hail Mary,
Full of Grace
The Lord is with thee."
I am here
My Mother is with me
"Blessed art thou
Amongst women."
She is the example
For how women

Should walk with grace
In the world
"And blessed is the fruit
Of thy womb, Jesus."
You are praising my name
"Holy Mary,
Mother of God,
Pray for our sins
Now and at the hour
Of our death."
You are asking my Mother
To pray for you
To me
And she does
So there is no shame
In this prayer
I hear these prayers
And my Mother
Prays for you
All the prayers of the world
Please God
Keep seeking His name
The Rosary
A lament of prayer
A cry for God's help
He walks amongst those who
Pray and seek him
The rosary is a gift
From God
Please pray….

Chapter 11
Family

God has walked me through a mighty storm. He has shown me many things and granted me many miracles. I cherish my family. I know that we are growing closer and stronger each day. I am truly grateful my family is together. The poem "Family" is about how precious they truly are.

"The Quilt" I wrote in memory of an elderly lady I met when I was a young adult working in a nursing home. She taught me how to make an around-the-world quilt. After my divorce, I began to do the things I loved again. Years later, I have finally finished the quilt and it reminds me of the happy and loving lady who taught me.

"My Daughter" I wrote after we were reunited. We just had a beautiful day. She was sitting on my bed talking about her day and our plans for her graduation party. I wrote this poem in gratitude for God seeing us through.

"Someone Came to Me in the Night" I wrote about my true love's father. Ever since he told me his father was dying, I prayed for God to shield him from the pain of the disease. The night he died, he came to me at 1:30 in the morning. Jesus was there. He touched me. He asked if I was all right. He brushed back my hair. I never met him in life. But his hand was like my true love's. I told him I was fine and that I could not stop loving his son and that God was protecting me. Then he was gone. I awoke. The next morning, I wrote this poem. When I drove by his parents' house, there were many cars. I knew he had passed.

Psalms 21:1-3: "The king shall joy in thy strength, O Lord; and in thy salvation how great shall he rejoice! Thou hast given him his heart's desire, and has not withholden the requests of his lips. Selah. For thou preventest him with the blessings of goodness: thou settest a crown of pure gold on his head."

Family

Family
Is precious
Bonds that are eternal
Family is where we
Feel comfortable and warm
Family defines
Who we are
Compassion and love
Wrapped in a beautiful
Gift of friendships and
Acceptance
Family
A circle of life
Unending
Worth more than
Gold
Family
The ties that
Bind us as one
That make us whole

The Quilt
Dedicated to Hazel Baylis

Many years have passed
Many tears have been shed
But in my heart
You have a place
So many things
You shared with me
Lonely and away
From your family
You still had a love
For life and people
Always there with a smile
And a kind word
Just sitting and talking
With you
I learned so much
The quilt you taught
Me to make
Will always bring me
Back to a time
In my life
Where you shared
A craft of love
For quilting
That I can now
Share with others
Many years later
The quilt is finally
Complete
There are so many

Memories of the times
We sat and talked
In this quilt
I shall cherish
The love it brings
When I think of you

Daddy, Are You Listening?

Daddy, are you
Listening?
Daddy, are you
There?
My heart is
Hurting
For I know
How much you
Care
Daddy, I am
Looking
To see what
I must do
Daddy, are you
Listening?
For I take
Direction from you
Daddy, I am
Worried
For the many
Burdens I bear
I saw how strong
You walked in
Life
I know how much
You care
Daddy, I need
Your guidance
Daddy, come

Rescue me
I am worried
I've lost my way
Daddy, you always
Listened
Daddy, you were
Always there
Daddy, please be
Near me
Daddy, please come
Quick
For my heart is
Hurting
For the one who
Knows I care
For everyone and everything
I know life is not
Fair
Daddy, can you
Hear me?
Daddy, are you
There?
Please come sit by
Me a while
And listen to
My strife
I miss you dearly,
Daddy
I owe you all
My life
For you were my
Rock

You were always
There
You could hold me
Tightly
Hugging me that you
Care
So Daddy,
Can you come to me
And sit a little while?
For I know that
When you're with me
I can find my
Smile
Daddy, I love you
Dearly
Daddy, are you
There?
Please, Daddy, are you
Listening?
Daddy, please
Draw near
For it is your
Loving daughter
Who calls for you
Tonight
Daddy, please come
Near me
And hold me
Good and tight!

My Daughter

My daughter is
A beautiful soul
I watch her each
New day
Arise with sleep in
Her eyes
To greet a brand-new day
My daughter smiles and laughs
And touches hearts with gold
She is lighthearted
And lovely
In each new path
She strolls
My daughter is
A lovely beauty
To behold
She reminds me
To let go of
The heavy load
I bear
My daughter
Smiles at me sweetly
Casting her eyes my way
As if to say
I love you and
Thank you for each day
My daughter shows
Love to every creature
She sees
Her heart runs

Wildly toward them
With affection in her
Own sweet, caring way
My daughter
Is a gift from
God
Who touches my heart
Today
I reflect knowing
She is a beautiful
Part of me
I know that I am okay
My daughter walks
Ahead of me
Venturing out in
The world today
She's happy that
The Lord has blessed
Her with a family
Today
My daughter teases,
Jokes, and plays
Tugging at my heart
For just to sit
And sip some tea
And pour out to me
Her heart
My daughter is so
Precious
No new gem
Can compare
She is a rare

Beauty
That lights a fire
In my heart
My daughter will never leave
My heart
She is always
There
For to have such a
Beautiful daughter
Gifted from above
Makes me feel
So loved
For I know my
Savior loves me
To grant me
So much…Love.

Someone Came to Me in the Night

Someone came to me
In the night
They are worried
About me
Deep asleep
In the comfort
Of God's arms
Someone came to
See if I was
All right
I felt their concern
For my wellbeing
Someone came
To me in
The night
I felt them
Brush my
Hair aside
And look upon me
Someone came
To me in the night
They love me
And wanted to know
I'm all right

Chapter 12
Revelations

I wrote "New Beginnings" with God's reassurance that the dark days will soon be over and there will be sunshine in my life again. Sometimes God is taking us on a journey to higher heights. We may think that we are not enough. We are not worthy. But God says we are worthy and we are loved. During a time of great frustration and doubt, God gave me this poem, "You Are Worthy!"

God is always reminding me there are rainbows in my life. He is reminding me of his promise. This summer my children and I went to "Pictured Rock." During the boat tour, God grabbed my attention. He painted a double rainbow across the sky. I thanked him. I was grateful for this time of happiness with my children. "Rainbows" is about God's promise to never forsake us.

When you are on a journey with God, he may show you a vision of where he is taking you. But sometimes it takes a long time to get there and you may fall down many times. It is these times that God is teaching you. God gave me "Press On" during one of those times. He wants me to never give up, and then you may have "The Perfect Day."

"Pass It On" is about our walk as Christians in life. God teaches us, guides us, and shows us many miracles. But he doesn't want us to keep it a secret. He wants us to "Pass It On," in our words, in our deeds, and how we walk like him in life. Others will see and pass it on.

Finally, God wants us to follow him closer, pray for one another, to be his hands and feet.

The book ends justly with:

Revelations.

New Beginnings

Begin each day
In words that say
All the love
In the way
I have taught you
Begin smiling and laughing
With a joyous heart
For your life has
A brand-new start
Begin singing and dancing
Give pause to the Father
For He is good
His love endures forever
Begin walking close to me
Care only what I think
Begin standing in the
Sunshine of my love
And I will rain down
Blessings from above.

You Are Worthy
(song)

You are waiting
There's nothing left to do
Anticipating
All of my promises to you
Today stand
Stronger than before
You're ready to do more
You alone are worthy
You alone are wonderful
Your beauty
Transcends all
Earthly things
You are waiting
For His amazing grace
Anticipating
Your joyous
Life
You alone are worthy
You alone are beautiful
Standing strong
In His amazing grace
He shows you
A wonderful life
Renewed
You are all
That God has meant
For you to be
Walking strongly
Holding on to thee

You alone are worthy
You alone are wonderful
His amazing grace
Has shown you
All that is anew
Believe in yourself
He will take you
To the Promised Land
Where beauty and wonder
Fill your life
You alone are worthy
You alone are beautiful
He takes you
To the highest heights
Amazes you with all of
These amazing sights
Your beauty
Transcends beyond you
He takes you to
A wondrous place
Where fear and doubt
No longer have a space
Your heart is full of
Joy and laughter
Every day is filled with
Forever after
You alone are worthy
You alone are wonderful
He takes you along a
Journeyed road
Where God's glory
Beneath the waters flows

You alone are beautiful
You alone are wonderful
He has raised you up
To the mountaintop
Look and see His glory
As He shines a light
Through you
To show His way
Be grateful
For all that is
From above
For you alone are worthy
You alone are wonderful
He provides for you
As you share His ways
In your life
Believe and have mercy
Forgive and believe
You alone…
You alone…
Are worthy!

Rainbows

Beautiful colors
Displayed in the sky
A promise that
Will not die
An extraordinary display
Of endless promises
God has given His word
To never forsake us
When you are troubled
Or in doubt
Look to the display
He paints across the sky
Beautiful colors
Of new life and freedom to be
The person He created
You to be
Stand strong
Stand in the light
Look up to the blue sky
Because after every storm
Comes the sunshiny rays
And across the sky
Shimmers the
Beautiful colors
Of new life
Rainbows!

Press into Me

Whenever you feel
Like you don't belong
Press into Me
Whenever you feel
Like things are all wrong
Press into Me
I will always be here
I will never leave you
Whenever you feel
You can't go on
Hold on to my hand
I will comfort and
Lead you
You are loved eternally
Enjoy this day
Enjoy the blessings
That will unfold
I am here
Holding you close
Your true love
Is coming
He loves and adores you
All will be as
Promised
Until then
Press into me!

Perfect Day

When I have a
Perfect day
I open my heart
And thank God
For it is by His grace
That this
Perfect day
Came to be…
From the beginning
Of this day
Full of blue skies
And happy thoughts
Until its ending
Where God revealed
Another long-awaited
Message
This day has been
Perfect
The love He has
Showered on me
Today from my
Children
The peace and
Harmony
That exists today
Lets me know
Of His deep love
For me
Today was a
Perfect day
Sent from above.

Pass It On!

I touch your heart
You touch the
Heart of another
Pass it on….
I offer my friendship
You offer your
Friendship to
A lonely soul
Pass it on….
I help you in
Times of trouble
You help another
In times of
Great trials
Pass it on….
I hug and comfort you
In times of great loss
And hurt
You hug another
Who has no one
Pass it on….
I walk in the light
Of the Lord
You walk in the light
Of the Lord
Others take notice
Pass it on….
I found God
And learned how
To walk with him

I shared it with you
Through me
You learned of
His word
You pass His word
On to another
Pass it on….
Jesus said…
Pass it on….
"Knock and the door
Will be opened."
Pass it on….
"I will never forsake you."
Pass it on….
"I love you."
Pass it on….

Revelation

Water
Life
Thirst
Word of God
Come to the Father
Drink of His word
All who are
Broken
Come to me
I am here
I am life
Through me
All things come
I am life
I am your Father
Through me
You can do
Anything
Come hold my hand
Walk along this land
I will show you
The wonders of all
Bring those who
Want to follow…
My soul
Thirsts to bring
All of you
To the Father
Walk
With me
And you will
Forever
Be free